The Forecaster Method

John Lincoln, MBA

Foreword

Digital marketing today is tough. CEOs don't see the business value of marketing until you prove it to them. Your sales team is constantly questioning the quality of leads in the pipeline and blaming your top marketing channel. Data privacy protections force tech companies to limit targeting options. Consumers are following suit and changing their habits – using voice search, turning to mobile first, implementing ad blockers, and choosing video over reading.

Times are changing rapidly and you have to have the intelligence, systems, tools, and foresight to adapt quickly. With these changing dynamics, you have to shift your mental framework and your identity as a marketer.

In the financial services space, a *fiduciary* is defined as someone with a moral and legal obligation to protect his client's investment. As the person in charge of demand generation and paid media, you must think of yourself as the fiduciary. You are duty-bound to make solid, safe investments that produce a positive return on ad spend. It is your ethical and moral obligation to never lose money.

You have a choice – you can drown in the complexity of the data. You can get lost in the dizzying pace of change from Facebook, Google, and every other emerging ad-tech platform. You can chase after the hot new thing like the frivolous, trigger-happy investor ready to throw your last dime at the next stock tip.

Or you can build a set of solid fundamentals and principles that carry you through – that no matter what changes come out in the future, empower you to evaluate your opportunities, and make the best decision for your company, every single time. This book gives you a framework, a system to make smart and confident decisions for your marketing investment.

I have great respect for the author of this book. John Lincoln has built one of the fastest-growing digital agencies in America by combining a keen ability to translate complex ideas into executable strategy with a sharp focus on the fundamentals, and a sincere passion for educating people about digital marketing. While some like to spin their wheels with theoretical nonsense, John keeps it dead simple. As Tony Robbins says, "complexity is the enemy of execution."

Your success and growth depend on your ability to execute and produce results. The *Forecaster Method* is your practical guide, your compass to empower you to focus on the activities that truly evaluate, forecast, and scale your digital marketing. If you follow the fundamental principles laid out in this book, your growth will not be incremental, it will be geometric.

Keenan Shaw

Director of Strategic Growth

Robbins Research International (Tony Robbins)

The Forecaster Method

Never Waste Another Digital Marketing Dollar Again (While Growing Your Business Faster Than Ever)!

The Modern System to Accurately Evaluate, Forecast, and Scale Your Digital Marketing.

What You Will Learn:

- Bring dollars online from traditional media with confidence!

- Accurately forecast and scale your digital marketing

- Establish goals and hit them while reducing costs

- Establish executive-level reporting and Key Performance Indicators (KPIs)

- Set the right overall marketing budget based on a real model

- Find new opportunities and phase out poor performers

- And more!

About The Author

John Lincoln (MBA) is the CEO of Ignite Visibility (a 2017, 2018, and 2019 Inc. 5000 company), a highly sought-after digital marketing strategist, frequent industry speaker, and winner of the coveted Search Engine Land "Search Marketer of the Year" award.

With 16+ years of demanding experience, Lincoln has worked with over 1,000 online businesses, authored thousands of articles, taken hundreds of websites to number one positions in Google for competitive keywords, built social communities to millions of members, and worked on many advanced projects in conversion rate optimization (CRO), search engine marketing (SEM), influencer marketing, media buys, email, Amazon, and affiliate marketing.

Lincoln is also the author of Digital Influencer, a book about digital marketing, and the producer and director of SEO: The Movie and Social Media Marketing: The Movie. Recently, Lincoln received the Most Admired CEO Award and San Diego's Top Business Leaders Under 40 Award from the San Diego Business Journal.

Lincoln has been featured in Forbes, Newsday, and The New York Times. He is an in-demand speaker, speaking at 2 events each month.

Lincoln holds an MBA, is Analytics and AdWords Certified, and loves to surf and play soccer. His mission is to help others through digital marketing.

Table of Contents

Introduction

It's too hard for me to watch anymore.

I can't stand to see you waste another dollar!

You're a Chief Marketing Officer (CMO), a Director of Marketing, a business owner, a startup. You're someone who is trying to make an impact on the world. You understand the importance of digital marketing in growing your business but aren't yet sure how to use it most effectively. Because of that, you're likely blowing money left and right, and you may not even realize it.

I get it. Digital marketing is complicated, and its many moving parts are constantly changing. But when you get it right, power, accuracy, and scale will follow.

In this book, I'm simplifying the process for you and sharing my formula for success for the very first time.

Why?

Because I want you to be able to scale your digital marketing for better results.

Because I want you to have a clear picture of what the correct digital marketing mix should look like for your business.

But really, because it's my purpose to help others through digital marketing.

I've helped thousands of businesses, been named Search Marketer of the Year by Search Engine Land, own a 3-time Inc. 5000 company which is one of the top agencies in the USA, and get to work with amazing clients such as Tony Robbins, Fox, 5 Hour Energy, Cox, and more.

I want to bring my knowledge to you.

Right now, marketers are bringing their money from offline advertising to online performance-based marketing programs faster than ever before.

In this book, I'm going to give you the framework to structure your program correctly.

This is your guide to managing millions of dollars in marketing, without waste, and scaling your digital marketing in the correct way to get you the biggest returns.

My system is called the Forecaster Method.

It's not a gimmick.

It's not a fad.

And it's not complicated.

It's a framework for looking at any digital marketing strategy.

It brings clarity to all things digital, puts them through a filter, and ensures you're only investing in the channels that make the most business sense for your brand.

With hundreds of ways to spend your money in digital today, now is the most important time for my system to be released.

Welcome to the Forecaster Method, your guide to transitioning more marketing dollars online from offline, structuring your approach, properly using a performance-based model, and using clear data to scale results.

If you are a CMO, business owner, or digital marketer (or perhaps aspire to be in positions such as these) of a multi-million or even multi-billion-dollar company, consider this book your new best friend.

As a large company you are competing with the smartest minds in the business, many of which are nimbler in performance-based marketing.

It is critical that you understand how to test, measure, and prove results as well as scale your online marketing. It is no longer the same marketing mix as it was a few years ago. Digital marketing has exploded and there are so many new ways to advertise it is almost impossible to keep up with.

The key to success is following a methodical digital marketing process.

By the end of this book, you will know what that process is and how to run a multi-million-dollar digital marketing program.

That is my promise to you.

I use this process myself and have done so for our clients whose revenues range from millions to billions of dollars a year.

That being said, I am going to need a few things from you so that you can make the most of what this book has to offer. As you move through this book, consider how the process applies to your specific needs and goals. Take notes and complete action items in each section. If you take the time to do this, I promise your revenue will climb online.

Sound fair? Great!

I will start off by giving you some basic, fundamental information that is crucial for you to know as a digital marketer. As we progress, I will get into more specific details and give you tools that you can utilize for success.

One last thing...

This book was intentionally kept incredibly short in order to focus on the Forecaster Method and how to build a digital framework that can be scaled.

I kept it clear and concise so as not to waste anyone's time. Some of the concepts in this book are business focused and others are marketing focused. Also, some of the topics are basic and some are advanced. It is quite a mix! But it is all information you have to know to be a true digital marketing master in the new world.

I 100% promise you reading every word of this book is worth your time.

Let's dive in!

Chapter 1: The Changing Digital Landscape

WHY IS ADVERTISING MOVING ONLINE FROM OFFLINE?

In 2017, sports apparel giant Adidas announced it would be packing up its advertising dollars, putting on its sneakers, and running from television to digital and social media advertising.

Why, you ask? The reason for this drastic shift in ad spending was to target younger consumers who predominantly use mobile devices for engagement.

In their annual report, Adidas CEO Kasper Rørsted explained to shareholders that digital touched the company at "every point along the value stream." In addition to increasing sales through digital engagement, the company was able to incorporate data which helped them continue to design, develop, and manufacture new products.

With a clear path in mind, Adidas is looking to more than triple their ecommerce revenue by 2020 and are hedging their bets that digital channels will help them get there.

But it's not only Adidas that sees the value in increased spending on digital advertising.

Nike has also realized that in order to keep up with their competitors online, increased spending on digital advertising is essential.

Always at the cutting edge of marketing, Nike upped their digital spending over recent years to not only increase sales but also to capture customer data. Through their online effort, Nike saw sales double in a two-year period and noticed that app users spend nearly triple what they do on Nike.com.

Similarly, American Express noticed a significant increase in customers when they focused their strategy on digital and social channels. In 2017 the company credited their digital efforts for 60% of its acquisition of 2.6 million new card members in their first quarter. The company also aims to increase their digital spending, as they see steady growth in new member acquisition and retention of existing customers.

Our company, Ignite Visibility, recently conducted a study of our own on the topic in February 2019. Here are some of the findings.

Key Digital Marketing Study Findings

Businesses under $1 million invest the most in social media, while businesses between $1 million and $5 million invest the most in search engine optimization, businesses between $5 million and $10 million invest most in online advertising, businesses between $10 million and $20 million invest most in email marketing, and those in the $20 million to $50 million and $50+ million range invest evenly between all channels.

Regardless of the size of the business, the majority will be shifting more marketing budget to digital. Businesses in the $20 million to $50-million-dollar range plan on shifting the largest amount to digital, with 90% saying they would be bringing more online.

The majority of businesses of all sizes find social media to be the most difficult channel to manage.

The larger the business, the more people responded they would be investing in all marketing channels, as opposed to just a select few.

Businesses $1 million and under had the largest number of marketers who did not know the digital marketing channel that had the highest return on investment (ROI). Larger businesses generally had a better understanding of channels with the best ROI.

As far as the type of content businesses would be investing the most in, video emerged as a front runner, but results made it clear that businesses would be investing in all types of content on some level.

As businesses grow in revenue, so does their budget allocation to all digital marketing channels (email, search engine optimization (SEO), social, paid, conversion rate optimization), marking a more mature business with a diversified portfolio.

They often start with social media, which is very low cost. Then, they graduate to search engine optimization and online advertising, and eventually build a list and work more on email marketing.

We also see that as businesses grow, they implement better tracking and develop a better understanding of the conversion rates and ROI around each channel.

About three years ago, businesses above $10 million in revenue spent approximately 90% of their budgets on offline channels, with only 10% being spent online. Now, especially for larger businesses, the pendulum is widely swinging closer to 60% online and 40% offline.

We do tend to see business size as a factor here.

Smaller businesses usually spend more online. The larger the business gets, the more they start to invest in offline channels and branding. Regardless, all sizes are shifting more of their budget to digital marketing.

I know the digital marketing statistics we just covered are a lot to digest.

Don't stress. First things first. It all starts with goals and that's exactly what I'm going to discuss with you in the next chapter.

Action Item

Write down your marketing budget by channel (traditional marketing, SEO, email, paid media, social media marketing, affiliate marketing, media buys, etc.). Does your marketing budget total 10% of revenue? Does your marketing revenue per channel match the numbers above? Save this for later and consider if you have the right mix.

Chapter 2: Goals and Conversions

START ALL MARKETING WITH A GOAL

No matter which digital channel you are going after, all successful marketing starts with a goal.

Why?

Well, because if you have a defined goal, you can lay out a strategy.

If you define a strategy, you can lay out a timeline.

If you define a timeline, you can lay out key performance indicators.

The sequence looks like this:

Goal > Strategy > Timeline > Key Performance Indicators

That is how to layout the perfect digital campaign.

Let's start off by defining what a digital marketing goal is. A goal is the desired action or event a user takes on a website. Your marketing goal could be anything from generating a specific amount of revenue for the year to capturing a certain amount of leads.

When it comes to digital marketing terminology for tracking the number of goals, there are three buckets:

- Micro conversions

- Macro conversions

- Brand awareness

Now, many people also add customer service as a bucket. But for the purposes of this book, we are going to leave it out.

Let's take a closer look at each of these goals and what they mean to your business.

CONVERSIONS

To better understand conversions, you first need to understand the different types of website models.

There are five main types of website models: websites for brands, customer service, ecommerce, lead generation, and news (I didn't come up with this list; it came from Google's Google Analytics course).

Each of the sites has micro and macro conversions, but they are different for each website.

For example, a lead generation site would look at email captures as a micro conversion and someone filling out the lead form as a macro conversion.

On the other hand, a news site would look at pageviews as a micro conversion, whereas someone clicking on a banner ad where they get paid on a per-click basis would be considered a macro conversion.

So, let's discuss *"micro conversions"* and *"macro conversions"* further. Generally, micro conversions are little conversions along the way to macro conversions, which are the ones that matter most to your business. Micro and macro conversions depend on the online business goals.

Micro conversions are actions customers take along their digital journey towards a purchase or whatever the end goal of your website may be. These micro conversions can be split into two types: process milestones and secondary actions. Process milestones are the successive steps towards a final (or macro) conversion. Secondary actions are desirable actions that indicate the potential of macro conversions but are not the primary goal of the site. Depending on the nature of your business, micro conversions may be actions such as viewing your "Reviews" page, visiting the "Request A Quote" page, placing an item in the cart, joining your newsletter, or commenting on an article.

Macro conversions are the primary goals of the website. The success of a website can be measured by these types of conversions. Macro conversions can be broken down into three categories: revenue-based, lead/member acquisitions, and inquiries. Examples of macro conversions would include such actions as completing a sale on an ecommerce website, completing a lead generation, or filling out a "Contact Us" form.

BRAND AWARENESS

Business Dictionary describes brand awareness as the "extent to which a brand is recognized by potential customers and is correctly associated with a particular product. Expressed usually as a percentage of target market, brand awareness is the primary goal of advertising in the early months or years of a product's introduction."

Clearly then, making sure consumers are aware of your brand is key to growing, scaling, and staying relevant in your industry. Generally, brand awareness is something businesses invest in once they have found a product fit, reach over $1 million in revenue or if they have a product or service where they need to create the demand.

Now that you know the types of marketing goals, you will need to decide which type of goal you are targeting with each digital marketing endeavor.

After establishing your goal, the next step is to know what different personas you will be targeting. A persona is basically a model of your potential customers. These might be people who are going to buy from you, channel partners, or even media personalities who you want to pitch to.

The most important thing to know about personas is that they need to be built around a goal. Simply put, you create a goal and then you create the personas that will allow you to achieve that goal. All of this background is important for context around the Forecaster Method.

Outline Your Objective

Before starting any marketing plan, make sure you outline the objective first. Establish what you are trying to achieve, whether it be revenue, leads, or something else. What number would you like to reach, and is that number reasonable? What is your budget? What will it take to get there?

I can't tell you how many times marketers embark on a strategy with no clear idea of what success looks like.

What does it look like to you? Is it $100,000 more in revenue, or $1 million? You need to know that before you start marketing, as your objective will dictate the strategy and the budget.

Once you determine your overall goal and what the projections look like, you will work backwards from there to bring it all together. While this

...ss may sound a little unorthodox, trust me on this. It will all start to come together and make more sense as I get into more specific strategies throughout this book.

Action Item

Write down your overall goals for macro conversions, micro conversions, and brand awareness for the year. For example:

1.   4,000 macro conversions (online leads)

2.   10,000 micro conversions (email captures)

3.   500,000 online searches (brand awareness)

A quick note on measuring brand awareness: the Forecaster Method is really a tool that should be used for performance-based marketing and macro conversions. However, it can be used for micro conversions and brand awareness as long as you have a revenue value to look at. Email captures are an easy micro conversion, but brand awareness gets a little tricky. Here are some ways people measure brand awareness:

1.   Number of searches for a brand online

2.   Number of brand mentions online

3.   Survey a segment of the population

4.   Share of voice (how much your brand is mentioned vs. your competitors)

5.   Overall traffic and reach for online assets such as website and social media

Chapter 3: Setting a Marketing Budget

WHAT DOES A NORMAL AD BUDGET LOOK LIKE?

There's really no such thing as "normal" when it comes to ad spend or budget.

While many companies rely on the textbook 10% of revenue as a rule of thumb, those confines don't necessarily fit every company's needs or goals.

In many cases, how much budget you allocate will depend on how you plan to acquire new customers, and there are many different ways to go about it.

You can acquire customers based on channel partners, 100% online, or through an acquisition strategy.

When it comes down to it, strategy is everything.

That being said, the model of 10% of revenue is about right. That means businesses under $5 million spend up to $500,000 a year on marketing, businesses under $10 million spend up to $1 million, businesses under $20 million spend up to $2 million, businesses under $50 million spend up to $5 million, and businesses under $100 million spend up to $10 million and so on and so forth.

I often say: create a marketing budget and strategy for where you want to be, not where you are now. Marketing will drive growth and the rest of the company has to step up and follow. Generally, keeping it in line with 10% revenue allows this to happen. If you don't scale your budget, you will stay in one spot and growth will slow.

Chapter 4: The Forecaster Method

What Is The Forecaster Method?

By now, you are probably wondering what the Forecaster Method actually is. Good news: you're about to find out.

As I go through the rest of the book, I want you to see how it applies to every single strategy I present.

The model of the Forecaster Method I am presenting in this book is a general one. Anyone can use this method to evaluate the value of any traffic online as a performance-based marketer would.

It should be noted that there are more specific forecasting systems for each channel. But this is the best method for the general marketer and business owner to use. The main reason is that it allows you to compare traffic channels to each other and select the one with the best return.

The Forecaster Method is a formula, but it is also a way of understanding marketing; it is a way of thinking about all the different marketing initiatives you take on.

It's actually very simple.

In its most basic element, the Forecaster Method looks at a source of traffic online, the target audience, the click-through rate, conversion rate, amount of transactions, value per transaction, cost per transaction, and the return. You can then use that information to make decisions and scale for the largest return.

The 8 Steps of the Forecaster Method

The Forecaster Method is comprised of eight steps. When put together, these steps will help you determine which channel (or channels) are giving you the best results, and which are lacking.

From there, you'll be able to make an informed decision on where to allocate your budget.

The breakdown looks like this: Source > Model > Forecast > Return on Ad Spend (ROAS) > Compare > Scale > Diversify > Optimize

Let's take a closer look at each step.

1. **Determine the Source.**

Your source is the individual source of traffic you are evaluating. In Google Analytics speak, a source is the origin of your traffic. In this case, it could be email, Facebook, Google search engine, a programmatic media buy, etc. To run the Method, choose one source to evaluate at a time.

2. **Build the Model.**

Once you've determined the source you're evaluating, you'll need to build a model to determine the actual number of conversions that source is bringing in. The model will look like this:

*Audience Size (the number of people you're targeting) * Click-through Rate (the number of people clicking on your search result, ad, email, social post, etc.) * Conversion Rate (the number of people taking the desired action on your site) = Number of Conversions*

Example

Audience Size of 300,000 * Click-Through Rate of 20% * Conversion Rate of 5% = 3,000 conversions

3. **Forecast the Value.**

Next, you'll need to forecast the actual value of your source.

To do so, you'll run this equation: Number of Conversions * Conversion Value to The Business (generally the lifetime value of the customer) = Value.

You should already have determined the number of conversions in the last step. The easiest way to determine the conversion value to your business is to look at your revenue per lead metric.

If for every 10 leads you generate $10,000 in revenue, you can assign a revenue per lead value of $1,000. Now, if you are an ecommerce site you would instead look at the average value of a transaction.

So, if you determined your number of conversions was 100 and your conversion value to your business was $1,000, your equation would look like this: 100 x $1,000 = $100,000.

Let's look at a quick real-world example. Say a company gets 10 leads. Out of those 10 leads, only one closes. That one lead which closed is worth $500. That would mean your revenue per lead equation would be 500 divided by 10, or $50. So every lead is worth $50 to the business in revenue generated.

$50 in revenue generated per lead is the actual value that the source is bringing to your business during the time period that you account for that revenue to the business.

4.   **Determine ROAS.**

ROAS stands for "Return on Ad Spend."

As the full name implies, it tells you how much money you're earning as a result of the amount you spend on advertising.

The formula for ROAS is simple: divide the total revenue you earned from advertising by the amount you spend on advertising (ROAS = Revenue Earned from Advertising / Advertising Expense).

For example, if you spend $2,000 on Google AdWords ads and earned $4,000 from people who clicked on those ads, then your ROAS is $4,000 / $2,000, or 2. In marketing terms, that 2 means 200 ROAS%.

Once you've determined the ROAS, you can begin to understand if the amount you're earning on each source justifies how much you're investing.

Using the example above, if the company spends $10,000 and generates 1,000 leads, and we know the revenue per lead value is $50, our equation becomes $50,000 / $10,000, equaling ROAS of 5, or 500%.

5. **Compare.**

You'll want to run the first four steps on each one of your sources.

Once you've done so, you can compare each traffic source side-by-side to determine which has the highest ROAS. Ultimately, this will tell you which of your sources is the most effective and delivering the highest returns. Don't worry, I'll break this down more soon…

6. **Scale the Best Sources.**

The channel with the highest ROAS is the one you want to focus on here. This is the one you should invest more in and scale to continue building revenue and hitting your goals.

This will likely mean reallocating some of the budget from your lower-performing channels over to the one with the higher ROAS for maximum growth.

Keep in mind, at some point all online channels have a diminishing return. Because of that, you will need to review each channel monthly.

7. **Diversify.**

While you want to scale the best channel for the biggest return, you also want to diversify your sources.

To do so, make sure to invest in four to six channels. You never want to have more than 30% allocated to one channel if possible; it is too much risk. Therefore, you should use the profits from your best-performing channel to build up other channels and to reinvest in further optimization. This is critical because in digital marketing, things change fast and there is always the risk of a channel disappearing. There have been many times in digital marketing when a large website like Google, Facebook, or Instagram makes a change that results in a business losing all revenue from that channel. If you are diversified, you can always pivot and ramp up in another channel. You will also know how much you need to invest if you know your ROAS.

8.   **Optimize.**

Optimize your conversion process to get a better return for your ad spend. This means investing in testing new audiences, new ads, new landing pages, new checkout processes, new post-conversion funnels, and more to determine what's most cost-effective. You always want to be working to bring acquisition costs down for each channel. I'm going to talk about this point a lot later in the book...

In marketing, we have to hit certain targets each year. We can use the Forecaster Method to scale our digital marketing channels to reach that goal.

For example, say your marketing goal is to grow from $40,000,000 in revenue a year to $44,000,000 in revenue, and you have the 3 following online revenue sources:

- Facebook Ads: $20,000,000 in revenue / $10,000,000 spent = 200% ROAS

- SEO: $10,000,000 in revenue / $1,000,000 spent = 1,000% ROAS

- Google AdWords: $10,000,000 revenue / $10,000,000 spent = 100% ROAS

So, if you need to grow by $4,000,000, you have the following options.

1. Spend $2,000,000 on Facebook ads

2. Spend $400,000 on SEO

3. Spend $4,000,000 on Google AdWords

What do you think your company's Chief Financial Officer (CFO) would want you to do?

This is the power of the Forecaster Method! It allows you to determine where you can spend your money for the largest return.

Based on this hypothetical model, you are clearly going to want to scale SEO as much as possible, as it gets the best return.

In fact, if the economy of scale stays the same, you might even want to consider investing more in SEO and pulling back on the other channels.

The Forecaster Method allows you to monetize your existing digital marketing channels and invest more into those with proven success. Furthermore, it can help you forecast a model for channels you haven't even started running ads on yet.

No more guessing.

No more blindly spending money.

Everything runs through a forecast and all channels can be compared against each other. This is actually exactly how I set up the dashboard for my own businesses and clients. It allows us to turn the levers on leads from each source.

In a nutshell, the Forecaster Method results in growth. The Forecaster Method takes the concept of Return On Ad Spend, a well-known metric in paid media, and applies it to all digital marketing channels. It also allows you to Forecast Return on Ad Spend for sources you have not invested in yet. This is an important point. With this framework, you can also set up clear digital marketing-based business models for new businesses that have not even launched yet. It allows you to go to market with confidence.

If you use the method along with generally accepted marketing principles, it looks like this:

1.   Scale marketing using model 10% of total revenue as allocation to business marketing budget (don't take your foot off the gas, keep scaling).

2.   Use profits from one marketing channel to fund the growth of additional channels and establish pipelines.

3.   Continue to scale your best channels and diversify, with never more than 30% of revenue coming from one channel.

4.   Allocate for awareness, consideration, conversion, nurturing, upsell, and remarketing in each campaign source. While not all traffic channels have these targeting abilities, you can use a multi-channel approach here. For example, if a lead comes in from a review site you can remarket to them on Facebook.

5.   Monitor each source's traffic, conversion rate, conversions, cost per conversion, conversion value, and return on ad spend.

6.   Every channel and source have a return on ad spend if you run the model based on revenue contribution to the business. Use that to weigh each against the other.

7.   Consistently test new sources each quarter with a pilot R&D budget to determine if they hit acceptable return on ad spend numbers.

8.   Establish 4 to 6 reliable sources to diversify and protect the business.

And that, friends, is how businesses grow in crowded markets!

This step-by-step process is how you set a strategy in the new world of marketing, with so many channels available to us and a major emphasis on the online consumer.

Action Item

Run the Forecaster Method on all of your online advertising. Establish ROAS and determine your most profitable advertising channel. Consider your budgets and whether it is possible to shift towards higher ROAS initiatives. Determine your marketing goal for the next year and consider the following questions.

1. Which advertising sources have the highest return?

2. Do any of your sources have diminishing returns?

3. Do you have a marketing budget that scales at 10% of revenue?

4. What is your goal for the next 12 months and which channels should get the most budget?

5. What is your perfect marketing mix to hit company growth goals?

The Forecaster Method makes marketing a financial model, which is exactly as it should be in the new digital age.

My business partner Krish Coughran and I have used this same method to scale our company to a 3-time Inc. 5000 company and into a $12 million+ business with only an initial investment of $15,000, which we saved and took from our own pockets.

We've also used this same model for our clients to assist them with their marketing planning. It's simple, it works, it makes sense, and I am happy I now get to share my system with you.

Let's look at another example.

In this example, we see there are 3 traffic sources. The business is spending $24,000,000 a month in digital marketing and generating $114,000,000 in revenue.

The business has ambitions to grow to $200,000,000 a month in revenue.

- Facebook Ads: $10,000,000 in revenue / $10,000,000 spent = 100% ROAS

- Email Outreach: $100,000,000 in revenue / $10,000,000 spent = 1,000% ROAS

- Twitter: $4,000,000 revenue / $4,000,000 spent = 100% ROAS

Based on the Forecaster Method, this business is too heavily dependent on email outreach for its revenue. They should be looking to add 1 to 3 more traffic sources and improve ROAS on Facebook ads and Twitter.

Their action items would be to launch a pilot program to test 4 new sources of traffic, determine the one that has the highest ROAS, and begin scaling that channel. They would also want to invest in conversion rate optimization and new ad creative for the Facebook and Twitter channel to drive those costs down. In the meantime, if they have the ability to scale email outreach further they can do that; however, it does make them even more dependent on that channel as a business, which puts them at risk. The main goal would be to get 4 to 6 channels generating similar levels of revenue to email outreach and with a ROAS that is acceptable to the business, which most likely would be over 200%.

To reach $200,000,000 a month in revenue they may choose a new short-term model such as this, which they eventually work to equalize more.

- (Keep spend same and work to improve ROAS) Facebook Ads: $10,000,000 in revenue / $10,000,000 spent = 100% ROAS

- (Scale slightly to take advantage of great return) Email Outreach: $150,000,000 in revenue / $15,000,000 spent = 1,000% ROAS

- (Keep spend same and work to improve ROAS) Twitter: $4,000,000 revenue / $4,000,000 spent = 100% ROAS

- (New Network) Google AdWords: $20,000,000 / $10,000,000 spent = 200% ROAS

- (New Network) YouTube Ads: $10,000,000 / $5,000,000 spent = 200% ROAS

As we can see above, we have created a new proposed model. This is something that can be shown to management and used to make decisions. All that is left is to execute.

While this is a good short-term model, it is not necessarily a good long-term model. What I would like to do now is help you generally visualize that progression of a digital marketing ad budget. I want you to know that this is not the same for all businesses. This is just a general framework.

New Business

Generally a new business starts by investing in one advertising channel and they have 100% of leads associated with that. Most times they will want to go low funnel with their advertising, meaning they want conversions, not awareness. So a new business advertising model will usually look like this:

Channel: Paid Media

- Budget Allocation: 100%
- Visitors: Near 100%

Rising Star

33

A rising star is a business that is profitable and growing. For the purposes of this exercise, let's say they are 6 months old and achieving $100,000 a month in revenue. At this point, a business will usually start with more channels such as content marketing, email marketing, social media marketing, and SEO. Now, these new channels are part of earned media, so they grow over time but start small. So a budget and traffic model might look like this:

Channel: Paid Media

- Budget Allocation: 60%
- Visitors: 65%

Channel: SEO and Content Marketing

- Budget Allocation: 20%
- Visitors: 25%

Channel: Social Media

- Budget Allocation: 10%
- Visitors: 5%

Channel: Email Marketing

- Budget Allocation: 10%
- Visitors: 5%

You might wonder why I chose these general visitor numbers. Here is the reason. The paid media will drive awareness that turns into larger visitors through SEO. Also, the content marketing and SEO work will start to slowly kick in and grow that visitor count. Social media often drives a small amount of visitors unless you are doing influencer marketing or have built a large community where people love interacting with your content. Social media traffic is more likely if you are a popular retail brand, celebrity, jewelry, lifestyle, or publication (or have a cool brand in an industry people are excited about).

OK, let's jump ahead and look at a mature model.

In this case, you are a 1 billion-dollar established business. What does the right marketing mix look like for digital specifically?

Pro tip: Put your top competitors into Similar Web or SEM Rush to see where they are getting their traffic from and their exact marketing mix. You can use this to recreate the same digital marketing plan for yourself.

OK, back to the perfect general model of the 1 billion-dollar business.

Paid Media – 20% Contribution To Business Leads

- Facebook
- YouTube
- Programmatic
- Display
- Google Ads
- LinkedIn

- Bing

- Instagram

SEO: 30% Contribution To Business

- Google

- Bing

- Yandex

- DuckDuckGo

Social Media: 10% Contribution To Business

- YouTube

- Facebook

- Twitter

- Instagram

- LinkedIn

- Niche Social Networks

Email: 20% Contribution

Referring Site Traffic: 10% Contribution To Business

- 50 to 100 Other Websites Sending Traffic

Affiliate Marketing: 10% Contribution To Business

- 20 to 200 Top Affiliates

Now you know the framework of a fully baked digital marketing model.

As a marketer and business owner, it is your job to push your digital marketing in this direction to the point where all these sources of traffic are working and generating revenue.

Let me briefly talk through why I set the framework up this way.

You will continue to invest in paid media; however, that revenue contribution as a percentage usually goes down as other sources grow and you build up your own audiences.

What happens is, you start getting returning visitors who come in through an organic Google search and you start to capture emails and market to them, so this builds the email marketing channel.

Your social following grows, and so does the press you get on other websites. This adds to your referring site traffic and your non-paid social media traffic. That is an important point – social media, just like Google, has paid and non-paid traffic.

You also will eventually do media buys on targeted websites. This is going to grow your referring site traffic.

Finally, there is affiliate marketing. Affiliate marketing has a black eye in digital marketing because many of the affiliates use spammy methods to make sales. That being said, you may choose to launch an affiliate program and pay a commission to anyone who sends business your way online. I've launched quite a few programs and have seen them go well when handled correctly. In a few cases, the affiliates actually became the main drivers of growth for the business. One quick word of advice, if you launch an affiliate program, start small and be selective. Don't just blast it out to the world. If you

open it up to everyone, as opposed to being selective, you run the risk of

damaging the brand. Vet your affiliates just like any employee or partner.

OK, back to the Forecaster Method.

Chapter 5: Understanding How the Forecaster Method Works with Analytics

Clearly, running the Forecaster Method will require the help of an analytics tool to track sources and conversion rates. Unfortunately, accurate tracking on a website is one of the most complicated topics out there. If you really get into how to accurately track on a granular level you can spend hundreds of thousands of dollars and a lot of time.

For the purpose of this book, I'm going to teach you the simple equation which I believe is 90% of what you need. However, if you really want to have accurate tracking online you need to work with an analytics company to set it up properly.

The good news is, almost all advertising networks come with their own analytics that give you audience size, click-through rate, cost per click, and conversion tracking.

However, even if they do not, analytics tools like Google Analytics have something called the sources report, which will show you all the different websites that send traffic to your website by default. It will allow you to view the traffic coming in, the conversion rate, and the number of conversions from each source. You do have to set up a goal or ecommerce tracking for this to work, but that is very easy.

From there, you can use Analytics to find all the information you need for the first 3 steps in the Forecaster Method: finding each source, building your model, and forecasting the value.

If you want to take things a bit further, you can get even better data by setting up campaign tracking.

According to Google, "In its broadest definition, campaign tracking refers to a method of identifying how users discover your site. Specifically, you use campaign tracking in Google Analytics to accurately track online advertising campaigns to your website, both from Google Ads generated campaigns as well as from other advertising sources."

Essentially, campaign tracking allows you a more granular view of your traffic sources. It can also allow you to aggregate all traffic into one area for a marketing campaign. For example, if you're running one creative ad on several different channels – Facebook, Twitter, and Instagram – setting up campaign tracking will allow you to see which platform is sending the most customers who convert on site, and therefore the most revenue.

While campaign tracking is undeniably useful, it's not essential for running the Forecaster Method. To do that, a basic understanding of analytics and metrics mentioned above will suffice.

Campaign tracking will allow you to track the most important data you want to associate with the traffic coming from your advertising channels.

Now, I said I would keep this part simple but I have to add a few quick points in case you were wondering why I said tracking is complicated.

First, you need to select an attribution model you are comfortable with. By default, you start with last click, meaning all the conversion value goes to where the last click came from. But, if someone found out about you through a blog post you wrote and then Googled you and clicked on a branded paid media ad, that is really not fair to give all of that conversion to that channel.

Paid media always often wants to use a weighted distribution model, meaning they apply more credit to certain things than others. SEO generally just wants to report on last click but will also take into account multi-channel funnels reports, which basically shows each traffic source that made a contribution to the conversion in order.

Affiliates and referring site traffic from media buys usually set up their own tracking solutions. Also, paid media always wants call tracking, which basically only attributes a call as a conversion if it goes over a certain length of time.

Here are a few more advanced tips.

1.   Yes, look at last click but also look at a liner and multi-channel funnel report when reviewing traffic.

2.   Do your best to integrate something called Off-Line Conversion Tracking. This means you track who actually becomes a customer, not just a conversion on your website. You can use this offline conversion traffic to refine your paid media strategy and get a better idea of who your customer is.

3.   Make sure you have individual KPIs tied to each traffic source. They are not all the same.

OK, moving on. We have a lot more to talk about. By the way, towards the end of this book we get into the most exciting topic... Basically, getting more while spending less and scaling.

Improving Your Lowest ROAS Sources

Now that you understand how to run the Forecaster Method and how it applies to scaling and diversifying, it's important to understand how to consistently improve conversions and ROAS. This is probably my favorite part of digital marketing.

Remember, the goal of the Forecaster Method is to identify which sources are most effective and invest in them accordingly. After all, the last thing you want to do is continue to shell out money on sources with small return. However, that doesn't mean you should neglect them completely.

Instead, you should look at ways to bring up their ROAS. This is why the last step in the Forecaster Method – optimization – is so important.

Quick side note, it has been my experience (and the general view of my digital marketing peers) that with enough dedication and the right strategy, you can make just about any established digital marketing channel work online… I generally define "established" as a network with millions of users a month that are your customers.

If you want to improve your ROAS numbers for a poor channel, you'll need to investigate each channel to find – and fix – any obstacles or breaks in the customer journey that may be keeping users from converting. For that, the use of analytics tools is crucial (this is assuming you have the 5 P's of Marketing down already – Product, Price, **Promotion**, Place, and People). I say that because good marketing can't really fix a poor business model.

Back to my point.

The best companies can convert traffic for less, and your goal should always be working to continually bring ad spend costs down while increasing the number of conversions. Remember, in digital marketing the cost for traffic goes up every day (the supply is slowly increasing while the demand is quickly increasing), so we must constantly be learning and getting better at new ways to reduce ad spend. The companies that win long-term will be those that convert for less.

Now, let's dive into some important analytical programs that can help you determine where you may be losing customers. While you may have heard of some of these before, I find that most people have no idea how to use them.

Good news – I'm going to tell you how to use them to decrease your marketing costs. I am not going to go through all the programs out there right now, just the ones that are relevant. We have an annual event called the Ignite 100 where we review and award the best marketing technologies each year, so this is something I spend a lot of time thinking about. I also taught digital analytics at UC San Diego for 6 years. I love this part of digital.

HEAT MAPS

Heat maps aren't new to digital marketing. In fact, they've been around for some time.

They're incredibly useful tools for diagnosing any website issues. The problem is, a majority of people still aren't sure how to use them to improve their website experience.

Essentially, heat maps allow you to see how users are interacting with your site or landing page. The "map" will show you where people spend the most time and what they scroll right by.

A couple of my favorite tools for heat mapping are Hotjar and Crazy Egg. Both allow you to see where the user is focusing on the page and can help give you a good idea of the user's main intent. If those things don't align with where you want them to focus, that information can help you modify the page in order to get more conversions from it.

One of the main things you should look for when analyzing a heat map report is a hot spot (or place someone is hovering) that is not clickable. Often, that means the user is trying to click the area to learn more but is unable to do so, signaling a disruption in the user experience. It can also mean they are spending too much time trying to figure something out.

Remember, as marketing continues to move more towards mobile, users want to act quickly. Along those same lines, you need to be splitting the data received from heat maps between mobile and desktop (by the way, I am going to give you a mobile conversion rate strategy later that will increase your conversions by at least 30%).

Because heat maps are a tool geared towards improving landing page conversions, they're critical to this method. Remember, the landing page attached to your ad is where any conversions will take place, so improving it will allow you to subsequently improve your return on ad spend.

A quick example of how I used heat maps to increase conversions:

I analyzed a heat map and saw a hot spot over some text. I read the text, and saw it said "awarded #1 by..." I realized people were trying to click on that text to verify the claim so I hyperlinked that text to a lightbox that discussed the award. Conversion rates jumped 15% overnight.

Action Item

Install heat maps on the most important pages and funnels on your website. Review them monthly for hot spots that are far away from calls to action on the page. Remove distracting hot spots and use the data to bring users attention to the main calls to action.

CONTENT ANALYTICS

Also in the name of converting traffic for less, you must use content analytics.

Content analytics are a little different than heat maps. Unlike heat maps, which show where users are focused on a page, content analytics show where the user actually clicked on the page.

In many cases, that information can be even more valuable than information obtained from heat maps. Content analytics will show you if someone (or many people) are repeatedly clicking on something that isn't actually a button, which would signal that you should consider making it a clickable link or turning it into a button.

Content analytics also show you if someone is clicking on something far too many times, such as a help button (lightbulb). If that's the case, the page itself clearly isn't answering their questions, and signals that it's an area you should consider modifying for better understanding.

For example, in a recent client study we saw that FAQs were one of the most popular elements on the client's web pages. However, they were the last link on that particular page. Because of that, we added even more FAQs and moved the FAQs higher on the page and immediately saw conversion rates increase by over 15%. When you think about it, that makes perfect sense. After all, if you answer all potential questions, users will be far more likely to sign up! This is the power of content analytics and the kind of insights they can give you about your landing pages.

Action Item

Review your content analytics each month and look for clicks taking place where they should not be on the page. If clicks are taking place on non-clickable areas, link that area to a target that will address the issue. If clicks are not taking place where you want them to be, find ways to emphasize your call to actions or refine your copy and images.

IN-PAGE ANALYTICS

Google Analytics offers something a little different than heat maps and content analytics: in-page analytics.

In-page analytics allow you to see the exact click-through rates on every single link on your web page. I love this report. It is so powerful and almost no one opens it. It baffles me. I'll bet even if you are an expert digital marketer reading this right now, you don't look at that report each month. Am I right?

So this report gives you click data and even highlights segments with the most clicks or the least clicks.

If you know the click-through rates and how many times people are clicking on those links, you'll be able to determine which links are the most important and powerful on your page, as well as which links are used the least.

One of my favorite things to do is look at the in-page analytics report for the website navigation. By doing so, you'll learn which of your pages are most popular in the navigation.

This information is extremely powerful. I often work on websites with millions of visitors a month, and if they don't have the right pages featured front and center in the navigation, they're leaving a lot of money on the table. It would be like owning a large retail store with millions of customers, but 90% of them didn't get to see your best product categories. Think about it: there's a reason Walmart doesn't feature their fishing products right when you walk in. Simply put, it's not what most customers are there to buy. Similar concept with your pages.

I recommend you take a look at that report and use it to restructure your navigation. You can thank me for the increase in leads or revenue later. This is one report people should be reviewing monthly and definitely taking into account regarding seasonality. People don't take enough time to look at these reports. With a little more focus you can improve ROAS and scale for less.

Action Item

Review in-page analytics for your home page navigation and readjust your pages from most clicked to least clicked, left to right. Remove any pages people are not clicking on at all. Review your top page's in-page analytics and look for the most clicked-on elements on the page and consider why and if it makes sense to emphasize those more. Review the items that are clicked on the least and emphasize them less.

TOP LANDING PAGES REPORT

Inside Google Analytics, there is something called the Top Landing Page report.

This report pulls the pages on your website with the highest traffic, which are the ones you must focus on to continually increase conversions. This is very important to ultimately improving your return on ad spend. This is probably the most important report in Google Analytics.

Generally, these top landing pages end up impacting each of the sources in the Forecaster Method on some level, which is why it's important to consistently review the sources of traffic coming to these pages. For each individual source, you should review the conversion rate, number of conversions, and conversion value.

For example, if you look at a top landing page and see that it has 100,000 visitors from Facebook and only 20 conversions, that's something worth investigating. People are clearly intrigued enough by your Facebook ad or post to click through to your landing page, but the page isn't doing its job to seal the deal.

At that point you should start evaluating how you can get more micro or macro conversion out of that traffic, whether it needs a stronger CTA, more engaging content, or stronger visuals.

It should also be noted that in Google Analytics there is something called a secondary dimension. This allows you to look at secondary sources of data. So, if you are looking at the top landing page report, you can next set a secondary dimension for source. What this will show you is all the sources of traffic that are coming to a landing page, how much traffic they are sending, and their conversion rate. This is so powerful! It can help you identify which sources do well with that landing page and which ones do not.

Using the Facebook traffic example, here is what I would do to diagnose the issue.

I would set a secondary dimension in Google Analytics and look at the landing page and the traffic coming from:

- Devices: This would be iPhone, Samsung, etc.

- Operating Systems: This would be Android, IOS, etc.

- Sources: This would be all the traffic coming to the page.

- Location: I would look at this on the country, state, and city level.

- Language: I would see what languages people speak who are coming to the page.

- Behavior: I would look at bounce rate and time on page.

- Flow: I would look at what page visitors went to after this page and try to see where they fell off in the conversion process. Google Analytics has an excellent report for this.

By that time, I would probably have some actionable items. Maybe the website is broken when viewed on a Samsung Galaxy and 4,000 of the visitors speak Spanish. So then we just fix the site and stop generating traffic from that language, translate the page, or put a clear auto translate button on the page.

Even more fun, tools like Sumo.com will allow you to detect the traffic source and serve pop-ups to only that traffic source. So if you wanted to, you could serve a pop-up on a landing page just to Facebook users offering 20% off, thus converting your traffic better.

Here is my internal checklist for how I evaluate a landing page. Match this to your own website, and you will see excellent gains.

- 7-second home page test – everyone should be able to answer the following questions when visiting the homepage within 7 seconds:

- What do you do?

- What problem do you solve?

- How are you different from everyone else?

- What action should the user take?

- Have a call to action on the page once on every screen size if possible

- Structure navigation from left to right with most important to least important items

- Navigation labeled based on visitor's understanding and needs

- Always have Contact Us in navigation

- Make sure there is a call to action above the fold on desktop and mobile on every page of the website

- Trust elements on homepage near top fold

- Each page should have a singular purpose

- Headlines should be user-centric, not brand-centric – speak to benefits, not features

- Items featured in the navigation should address each of the top visitor personas – as identified by persona mapping

- Clear panel/section headings

- Consistency in button and link visual treatment

- Clear page titles (for non-homepages)

- Strategic use of color and visual elements (size, shape, position, color, contrast, motion) to guide visitor, not distract them

- Ease of readability

- Contrast of text when on images

- Size of font

- Keep full-width copy-sized font to a minimum

- Hero images that support messaging, benefits

I could go on, but this is a great start for any landing page.

Action Item

Review all top landing pages and put a plan in place to increase micro or macro conversions for every source of traffic. Set a conversion rate goal for the website and work to hold all landing pages accountable for that goal. For example, it could be a 2% conversion rate for macro goals and 8% conversion rate for micro goals.

Your action plan could be something like (and I recommend this) adding a call to action above the fold on each page and putting in place a program to split test copy and images (Optimizely or Google Optimize are great tools for this). Also, consider firing a pop-up on each top landing page after three seconds asking visitors to call or click a button for a special offer.

And stop, I don't want to hear you say you hate pop-ups. Everyone says that and they try to write them off as spam. You hate them because you don't know what you don't know: they get massive results and can be used responsibly. Correct pop-up implementation usually increases conversions 15% to 30% and actually helps the user in the process.

TOP EXIT PAGES

Your top exit pages report will tell you where you are losing most of your visitors. But that doesn't mean you should discount these pages – they're also extremely important for conversion rate optimization.

To see an increase in conversions, I recommend you fire an exit pop-up on these pages. You will get around a 1% to 5% click-through rate on that pop-up and start making more sales immediately. Depending on the content, these are also great pages to either add related articles if you are a news site, or a call to action or product if you are a lead generation site or ecommerce site, respectively.

Action Item

Review your top exit pages each month and ensure you have action items in place to reduce exits and increase conversions. We will talk more about how to do this in the next section.

Bonus: POP-UP ANALYTICS

Pop-ups come in many forms. Some fire after a visitor spends a few minutes on your page, while some pop up as someone tries to leave your website. Some great pop-up tools such as SumoMe or OptinMonster allow you to fire and split test them to see which ones are going to be the most successful for conversion.

There are many different ways to fire pop-ups – and I've tried most. The full-page takeovers have the highest conversion rates, but they really bother users (and I don't recommend them because they are too aggressive). The pop-ups that fire in the middle of the page out of nowhere also bother users, but they are less invasive and generally do very well to convert users. I leave it up to you if you want to use this one. I generally do.

My favorites right now are the scroll down pop-ups, timed pop-ups, and exit pop-ups. I like to set the scroll downs so the user sees the pop-up when they scroll down 1% of the page. It's a good idea to have them come in from the bottom right, and the content should be helpful to the user and related to the content on the page. Whatever the content on that page is helping with, the pop-up should be the next step in that process regarding the product or service you offer.

If you want to take it a step further, you can integrate with third-party tools like a Drift chatbot or Clearbit. Drift will allow you to create an automated dialogue flow with your users and Clearbit can enhance the data and allow you to personalize the messages. It is a powerful combination. These tools are really good for companies in the B2B space who like to work mildly warm to cold leads.

Action Item

Here is my framework for pop-ups.

Pop-ups

- Photo of a person if possible

- Nudge pop-up 1% down the page

- Standard pop-up fires after 3 seconds

- Pick a pain point for the user and provide a solution and then give a call to action

- Run a split test on a monthly basis

- Pop-up can capture email or redirect to landing page

- Recommend pop-ups for highest traffic landing pages that are custom

- Recommend creating general pop-ups by segment of your website

Chapter 6: Creating an Online Sales Funnel

Now that you have a much deeper understanding of your customers, how they behave, and how to track their behavior, you are ready to map out a marketing strategy that works for you.

Remember, the Forecaster Method will help you identify which channels are working best and where to allocate more of your budget, but each channel is just one part of an overall strategy. They all need to work together to form one overarching sales funnel that pushes users to your goal.

Keep in mind, it works like this: someone uses a device (phone, TV, tablet, refrigerator, whatever – it's now the age of the Internet of things); they interact with a browser, assistant, or app; and they either convert right there or they take the next step in the app, assistant, or website. They then either convert there or turn into an audience. Audience is a powerful word which we are going to tackle pretty hard soon.

You need to think about every step deliberately and make sure it forms a clear path to your conversion goals.

In this case, it helps to make a storyboard, map it out step-by-step, and consistently work to make it better. Your analytics will tell you where people drop off in the funnel. Make sure you're reviewing consistently and fixing any problem areas on your website.

One thing that almost all businesses forget to do is draw out what their perfect customer journey looks like. When I say this, I mean not only from a marketing perspective but also from the perspective of increasing customer lifetime value. Both work together. How many products or services can you sell to a customer? What sequence do you sell them in? How long do you need to wait before selling them more? What is the marketing strategy around each sale? Think about this for your own business.

Collect Email Addresses

Collecting email addresses is considered a micro conversion and can be a goal of the Forecaster Method and part of the model.

Here is an example of how that looks.

You capture 1,000 email addresses and it costs you $1 to acquire each one.

In your email blast, you have a click-through rate of 20% and a conversion rate of 10%, giving you 20 conversions.

Your revenue per conversion is $5,000 (20 conversions x $5,000 revenue per conversion), giving you a return of $100,000.

Your cost to run the email marketing campaign is $10,000.

$100,000 in revenue divided by $1,000 (to acquire the emails) + $10,000 (to run the campaign) gives you a return on ad spend of 909%.

This allows us to see that this is a high-yielding endeavor. Scale!

As you can see, capturing emails and running email marketing can pay large dividends, at least in this model which is similar to those I have seen for B2B.

Collecting email addresses can result in a large return through email blasts, but an important point of improving your ROAS for any channel is nurturing the customer.

As we move through this book, I am going to talk about more ways to get the most out of your current audience. One of those ways is the drip campaign, aka automation.

The Drip Campaign

A drip campaign is a slow and steady series of emails that you send to prospects who have provided you with their email addresses. The idea is to build a relationship slowly over time until the prospect is comfortable making a purchase. It should be noted that there are many different cases for drip campaigns / automation.

Here are some example automations with email:

- Educational emails with links to blog posts

- Follow-up emails sent to prospect after form is filled out

- Post-purchase transactional emails

- Lapsed customer reactivation emails

- Lapsed prospect reactivation emails

- Event-triggered email series

What the real pros do is align their drip email marketing campaigns with other marketing channels. For example, instead of just sending them an email, also send a text message and remarket to them on the Google Display Network, LinkedIn, Facebook, Instagram, YouTube, and more. All with the same message.

When you do this, it will improve the ROAS of each channel and allow you to convert for less. Once you have made any contact online, you have to nurture it. In marketing there is something called the rule of 7. If a customer sees your ad or content 7 times, they often become a customer.

Here's what a typical drip campaign might look like:

Day 1 - send a "welcome" email that thanks the prospect for showing an interest in your product or service and offers them a video to watch about why you are the best company (I love this strategy, it can really warm up a lead).

Day 2 - send an email that offers the prospect a freebie, such as an e-book that contains information relevant to people in your target market.

Day 3 - send an email that includes a customer testimonial about your product or service.

Day 4 - send an email that includes a personal story that will help people in your target market become more successful.

Day 5 - send an email that goes for the "hard close" with a special offer.

After Day 5 - Send monthly content marketing emails to them, special offers, and invitations to events.

Etc.

Drip campaigns can do an excellent job converting shoppers into buyers.

Pro Tip: After someone fills out a lead form, make sure the next page you send them to is not just a simple thank you page. Put a video on that page that further sells them on the product or service. This will help your close rates. Every step in the funnel matters. Also, send that same video to them via email.

Action Item

Review your online lead generation or ecommerce system and make sure you have an automation campaign and remarketing campaign attached to it. If a user abandons your funnel, landing page, or check out process, fire a pop-up that offers them something in exchange for their email address. Make sure you get those people into a drip system as well. Shoot for an email capture rate of 4% to 10%.

Take into account the following:

- Email automation campaign
- YouTube remarketing
- LinkedIn remarketing
- Google display network remarketing

- Instagram remarketing

- Gmail remarketing

Chapter 7: Creating Clear

Reports and KPIs

In order for the Forecaster Method to be effective, you need to be able to track the framework in real time – monthly, quarterly, and annually. That's why it's so important you have KPIs and the right reporting set up. Here is how I like to do it.

Track, Report, and Refine KPIs

Your key performance indicators (KPIs) are what tell you whether or not you're effectively hitting your business goals.

How they're defined will depend on your business objectives. It could be an increase in sales revenue or an increase in qualified leads, for example.

Whatever they end up being, they should be tied closely to your business goals and monitored closely.

Consider reporting KPIs with a real-time format, such as Google Data Studio dashboard.

The first tab of that report should show traffic, conversion rate, and conversions by traffic source that are tied to your KPIs. This will allow you to see how many conversions you are getting from each source of advertising that you are paying for.

You should put in a conversion value in your analytics program. If you have a lead generation site, you just put in a number that says how much that conversion is worth. For ecommerce, you use the transaction value. This will show you how much each source is worth to you.

Start with a few months of benchmark data. Eventually, you will be able to look at this report over time and get some excellent data.

Action Item

Create a Google Data Studio dashboard and connect it to your Google Analytics or any other analytics tool. Develop a sources report and a channel report so you can track your data in real time – daily, monthly, and in any other duration you like. Make sure the report shows new visitors, goals, and goal value. This would be transaction and transaction value for ecommerce and a bit different for a news or branding site.

Why You Need a Marketing Report

Reporting is one of the most important ways to provide your team, investors, and/or clients with the successes and challenges in your marketing process. It is through the information included in your reports that CEOs and other executives make informed decisions to advance the company.

The Forecaster Method simply cannot continue to be effective without reliable, updated reports along with analysis that prove the value and ROAS of each source you choose to invest in. Strategic decisions should be made on a quarterly basis based on these reports.

What to Include In Your Marketing Report

If you are reporting to a CEO or CMO (or just want to run the most efficient program for yourself), you are going to need an executive report that aligns with the Forecaster Method system.

Here is a general outline you can use that is a surefire hit! You can build this all in Data Studio, another dashboard, or do it manually in PowerPoint.

- Executive summary (200 words or less, summarizing the current state of all the marketing)
- What was done during the period
- All traffic channels/sources, year over year
- All traffic channels/sources, month over month
- Top performing creative
- Organic SEO, year over year
- Organic SEO, month over month
- Organic SEO start of campaign until now, with annotations
- All keywords ranking in search engines
- Top keywords ranking in search engines
- Top keywords vs. competitors index report
- Social media sources traffic, month over month
- Social media sources traffic, year over year
- Paid media sources traffic, month over month

- Paid media sources traffic, year over year

- Affiliate sources traffic, month over month

- Affiliate sources traffic, year over year

- Referral sources traffic, month over month

- Referral sources traffic, year over year

- Email sources traffic, month over month

- Email sources traffic, year over year

- Custom digital initiatives

- Integration with offline initiatives

- Strategic plan

Action Item

Develop a reporting template based on this outline. Customize it to your individual business needs. Note, this can all be done in Data Studio (and other reporting tools), or the data can be custom gathered from the marketing tools you are using.

Chapter 8: Why Audiences are the Future

Now I want to talk more about where things are headed and bring this all together.

It is my belief that audience creation is one of the most important strategies businesses will be looking toward over the next 5 years.

The reason? You've spent all this time and money to generate traffic to your website from TV, radio, email, SEO, paid media, social media — you name it! — but now we can develop clear audiences based on people who have visited the website (or parts of the website) and target them over and over again, in the exact way we want!

Many companies have a decent grasp on digital marketing and are actively working on a strategy that includes the common sources. Those strategies are critical, no doubt, but it may be worth adding another strategy into your cross-channel mix: audience creation, management, and marketing.

I have to talk about this here in the context of the Forecaster Method, as it is one of the main ways to cut your customer acquisition costs over time.

An audience is a group of users that you can target. Some audiences you own and others your rent or build in other networks.

See, Google Analytics Audiences (as well as Facebook audiences, LinkedIn audiences, Quora audiences, YouTube audience, Pinterest Audiences, etc.) provide an in-depth look at behavior, acquisition patterns, and conversion rates, as well as the demographics, interests, and more of those people who come to your website. Now, they all work in different ways and offer various insights into how the customer interacts on their ad network and your website.

It's beneficial to be acquainted with your audiences because they become a well of revenue potential you can draw from as needed.

You can fine-tune your messaging to each group and move them through the sales funnel and customer journey by understanding their goals. The benefits are two-fold here: get your audience right and you'll deliver better messaging and get more mileage out of your marketing dollars.

The end result: better ROAS and the Forecaster Method system begins to convert for less.

Today, the importance of personalized messaging and targeting can't be overstated.

Analyzing your Audience report allows you to gain valuable insight into your audience characteristics and craft your ads accordingly.

What is the Google Analytics Audiences Report?

Nurturing users and knowing your custom audiences is critical to the Forecaster Method. For example, you might have a 90-day remarketing audience on YouTube that only has people who have visited your contact page. You know with that audience you get the highest click-through and conversion rates. If you get down to a point where you really need conversions, you can target this bottom of the funnel audience and get conversions for less. You know that your ROAS for this lower funnel audience is much higher than a top of funnel audience, such as a general display category audience.

That is why I want to take a little time to teach you about Google Analytics' audiences and how they work. As I go through each of these, think about your own business and what it would look like if you ran ads on each of these, calculated ROAS, and ran them through the Forecaster Method. That is another important point: the Forecaster Method can be done on the audience level as well. In fact, that is the best way to look at it on a micro-level;

meaning, the Forecaster Method does not need to be done by channel, medium, or source. In digital marketing, you can keep drilling down until you find the area that is unprofitable. So in a Google Analytics' audience for paid media targeting, you can look at the audience and all the subgroups of that audience such as location, gender, age, income, and more.

With Google Analytics, there are endless sources of insights about who visits your website, reads your content, and buys your products.

Google provides a handful of pre-configured audiences, or you can build your own from scratch. As a quick point of reference, an audience represents a segment of users who share some common characteristics.

Where Do You Find Your Audience Report?

Before we start talking about how to grow your audience with paid media, you'll need to know where to find them.

All of your audiences can be found in the Audience Manager. To look at the audiences report, navigate to the Audience tab inside your Google Analytics dashboard.

Then, select audiences.

You'll then see a general report that lists all of the audiences you've chosen to follow.

If you've never used the tool, you'll see that Google has done a bit of work on your behalf.

You'll notice a few basic remarketing campaigns are already there: All Converters, All Regular Site Visitors, and Similar to All Regular Site Visitors.

What are these?

Well, All Converters is an audience of all the people who have converted on your website.

All Regular Site Visitors is an audience of everyone who has come to your site.

Similar to All Regular Site Visitors is an audience of people who share the characteristics of people who have visited your site, but have not been there before.

You have the ability to run ads to each of these audiences.

How to Create Google Analytics Audiences Based on Data

To populate the Audience report with data, you'll first need to enable the Demographics and Interest reports and create an audience. Use one of the pre-set options within the Analytics dashboard or create a new audience from scratch.

Below, I've included a list of the datasets you can use to inform your custom audience.

Demographics

Demographics represent the age and gender composition of your website traffic. On their own, this might not be all that useful. However, when paired with other insights like what channel they came from or interests, they can play a valuable role in informing your messaging.

For instance, if you're noticing a lot of women between 18-24 found your site through Instagram and are interested in fashion, you might aim for a younger and less formal tone. Taking this a step further, you might push this audience to a specific landing page on your website and then build a remarketing audience from it. You can then run ads to that audience, see it if converts, and if it does, perhaps create a similar audience.

Interests

Interests represent what's known as "psychographic" data, which covers shared personality traits, beliefs, and attitudes.

Interest data is vital to advertisers as it can be used to help you focus your ads and content topics based on what your audience cares about.

Geo

Geodata represents the location breakdown of your audience. This comes into play if you're doing business on a global level, as you may want to break down your ad campaigns by country or display ads to different audiences during different times.

What's more, the virtual map gives you the information needed to create seasonal ads or locally-focused content.

Over time, this data can be used to uncover which areas drive the most traffic, spend the most money, or have the highest conversion rates.

Behavior

The behavior section breaks down your audience by reviewing how often people visit your site, which pages they look at, and how long they spend on specific pages.

Typically, behavior metrics are used as a way to gain an understanding of how well your content is performing. However, sales and ecommerce teams can use this data to inform their business goals.

As you begin looking at user behavior, try to understand what visitor behavior leads to a conversion.

Enable Benchmarking

I love this report. It gives you the basis for how you are doing. Let me explain.

Enabling benchmarking on Google Analytics means that you're allowing Google to share your data anonymously. In exchange, you'll gain access to a more granular set of industry categories and data, allowing you to dive deeper into geographic information, traffic breakdown, and more. It will also give you traffic levels for your industry so you can see how each of your traffic sources is stacking up to the industry. They don't give you conversion rates for each channel, so you will have to use your best guess there.

How to Create Custom Google Analytics Audiences

According to Google's Support documentation, the pre-built audiences should cover all of your targeting bases. However, you'll get more out of this report by customizing.

The reason being is that every business is different and companies are likely to see better results by mixing, matching, and excluding metrics based on their unique audience profile.

For example, you can connect information from the behavioral insights report, then target specific interests and get more specific location-based data.

To create an audience, you'll need to sign into your Google Analytics account.

Click Admin, then navigate to the property where you wish to create the new audience.

From there, click Audience Definitions > Audiences and Add New Audience.

Once you're in, you'll have several audience segments to choose from. Examples include All Users, Smart Lists, Returning Users, Users Who Have Completed a Transaction, and more.

After you've selected an audience or multiple audiences, you'll then want to publish them to your Ads page by selecting Ads as the destination for each of your audiences. This way, when you go to create your pay-per-click campaigns, your audiences will be there next time you log in.

Action Items

Put in place a remarketing strategy for each network you are on. Make sure you have a series of remarketing ads that serve over a 90-day period. Each set of remarketing ads should be in a sequence that nurtures the user and individual ad creative should be tailored to the network and demographic. Organize your remarketing audiences based on what has the biggest return for the business. Make sure any data you collect is reflected in your privacy policy.

How to Use Different Types of Advanced Audiences

We have talked about using visitors who come to your site or interact with your ad to create an audience. Now let's talk about an audience Google has made which has not interacted with you yet.

As we've mentioned, Google provides several "pre-set" audience types that you can use to inform your campaign. You can combine these audiences, or create a new one from scratch.

Let's look at a few of these audiences just so you are aware of them and in case you want to test them for your paid media forecast model. After that, we will wrap up with some very important points about what to look for to measure success in each channel.

Life Events

As of now, AdWords supports the following life events:

- About to graduate college

- Recently graduated college

- About to move

- Recently moved

- About to get married

- Recently got married

On its own, Life Events may or may not be relevant to your industry, but this advertising segment is growing. Essentially, you can target people based on things that are happening in their life. We determine this based on what they are doing online.

Affinity Audiences

Affinity audiences are based on topics of interest. Google collects data as users engage with different types of content – YouTube videos, pages, ad clicks, articles, and more.

It's worth noting that you can customize affinity audiences to fit your brand and business goals better.

Remarketing Lists for Search Ads

RSLAs allow you to customize your search campaigns based on user behavior of your past website users. That info can then be used to tailor campaigns around those audience preferences while they're searching on Google.

Activity-Based Remarketing

Activity-based remarketing efforts aim to promote your pay-per-click ads to people based on specific actions. So in this case, your best bet is to create marketing funnels in Google Analytics that correspond with your sales funnel.

For example, you could create an audience based on the pages they visit –are they checking out pricing? Are they reviewing case studies or how-to guides? These people are likely interested in buying from you, but may need more information before pulling the trigger.

Customer Match

According to Google, Customer Match allows you to combine your online and offline data to re-engage your audience across Search, Shopping, YouTube, and Gmail.

So, where does growth enter the equation? How it works is, Google uses the information that your customers have offered up about their lifestyle, demographics, and habits, and targets people with a similar audience profile.

A few ways you can use customer match to drive both awareness and sales:

• Connect with new audiences on YouTube by targeting people similar to your "conversion" audience.

• Create Shopping and Search ads based on existing customer behavior. In this case, you might want to target people similar to your most frequent shoppers or biggest spenders.

• If you go the Gmail route, you can promote a special offer to audiences that match your existing customer profiles. New customers will see your ad displayed in that search bar on top of their inbox.

In-Market

In-market audiences are used to help you find people who are already researching products or shopping around for the best price.

As you develop a custom audience, in-market may be worth including alongside other audience profiles, especially if you're running a search display or shopping campaign. I love this targeting and use it all the time.

Similar Audiences

Similar Audiences are a lot like customer match but are used to inform remarketing efforts inside of Search, Shopping, Gmail, and YouTube.

How it works is, Google reviews search activity happening at the same time users are being added to your remarketing list.

As a point of reference, the people on your remarketing list have already spent time on your site. They may have abandoned a shopping cart or spent time looking at products within a specific category.

Google's algorithm looks for potential customers with similar search behaviors to those people on your remarketing list.

Action Item

Review all the new audience targeting abilities for each of the major networks. Integrate them into your performance-based marketing program and build out micro Forecaster Method Systems within each ad network. Continue to use the Forecaster Method to evaluate how you are spending money within each network. Continue to capture data and set up audience-based advertising strategies based on the behavior of the highest revenue-driving users who have been to your site.

Chapter 9: Deeper Insights Into Each Channel

In this book, I did a deep dive into the Forecaster Method, conversion rate optimization strategies, Google audiences, and some digital marketing data. I tried to stay away from telling you this is exactly how to set up a SEO, Facebook, email campaign, etc., and instead tried to stay specific and focus on data and forecasting. The goal is to get you to think of all digital as performance-based and to give you the framework to measure it. This is a system I use to cut marketing budgets by 10% to 30% while improving return on ad spend. We can then use that money to reinvest and scale the business. It works!

In this last section, I'm going to cover what to look for in each of these channels at a high level. My hope is that it helps Chief Marketing Officers,

Directors of Marketing, and business owners know what to look for and see the channels through expert eyes.

Paid Media

In paid media, you want to look at your cost per acquisition and ROAS. You have to know how much you are willing to pay for a lead or transaction for each business unit. If you know that, it will allow you to clearly measure the effectiveness of each paid media source. In addition to that, you need to know how many of the conversions are quality. When you start to look under the hood, your next important items to look at are your top performing creative, best audiences, and how you are targeting users at each stage in the funnel, from awareness to interest to decision to action to remarketing. You can actually put each of these levels through the Forecaster Method and run a mini-business model on each network, asset, and audience. That is what I love about digital!

Email

Email marketing is often neglected by businesses under $2 million. But when they get bigger, they start to really realize the power of it. Large businesses invest significantly more in email because they understand the return and often have more customer email addresses. With email, it all comes down to your list-building strategy, list size, open rate, click-through rate, and conversion rate. If you are able to get these metrics, it will allow you to run a forecast and have a great idea of the business model. From a Forecaster Method perspective, if you spend $100,000 on email each year and make $1,000,000, you would have a ROAS of 1,000%. You can then use this to weigh against the other mediums and determine where to spend money for the largest return under the Forecaster Method.

Social Media and Social Ads

I've seen businesses built 100% off social media ads. Facebook, Instagram, LinkedIn, YouTube, Twitter, Quora, and others all have the ability to build a business if you put in the time to figure them out, and the business is a good match. I love some of the businesses lately that are only built off one very good Instagram ad. You will often see one amazing ad with 10 million views and amazing creative. That one ad drives a whole business off of a Forecaster Method model! In most cases, people quit these networks too soon. You need specific tracking and pixels for each network, as well as creative content that is unique to the network, and a landing page or funnel. Running the Forecaster Method on any social ad spend is cut and dry. These should be part of your marketing mix. The old days of social media without ads are gone unless you are famous on some level or have media power. You have to spend on social now.

Organic

Your organic channel report is where you will see traffic for Google, Bing, and other search engines. Generally, you should shoot to increase traffic here 20% to 50% year over year depending on your budget and maturity of the site. When you open this tab, you want to see new users up year over year. Your growth here will be dependent on your SEO, content marketing strategy, and growth of your branded searches. One thing that is very important is that if this report is up or down, you can easily find out why by looking at the top landing pages and applying a segment for organic traffic. This will show you where the drops and gains are. Most people do not understand that when it comes to search engine optimization, your website is really a diversified portfolio of traffic. Every website should be looked at in segments, as some areas are more important than others. By the way, if you want to learn more about SEO I have published over 100 free SEO classes, created by myself, on the Ignite Visibility YouTube channel. Go there to get a free master's degree from me in SEO.

Affiliate

If you are not familiar with affiliate marketing, it is usually one of the last places most businesses turn for online marketing. Generally, it's a good idea to start with paid media, email, social media, SEO, referrals, display, and then get into affiliates last (I said generally). Now, building an affiliate network is different than creating referral partners and pipelines. That is traditional business development and should be done as soon as possible. With affiliate marketing, you are using a service like Commission Junction or Affiliate.com to sign up for an affiliate network. You give them ads and they offer them to other websites to run for a commission. This sounds great, right? But it is often much harder than it seems, mostly because it is very hard to find quality affiliates willing to dedicate time to your offer. Most networks have sign-up fees and management fees as well. When looking at this opportunity in regards to the Forecaster Method, it is pretty cut and dry. Take your total revenue divided by your cost to run the program (don't forget about affiliate fees here). Of course, as I explained earlier you could also take this down a level to the affiliate, another level to their channels, another level to their sources, etc.

While we haven't talked about the below channels yet, they are just as important to measuring performance and improving return on ad spend:

Referral

In your referral category in Google Analytics you will find all the websites that are sending traffic to you that have not been set up properly in campaign tracking. This report is a gold mine. What you want to do is look at each of the sources, find the ones with the highest conversion rates, and look for opportunities to scale those initiatives (spend more money with the highest converters for the lowest cost). Often, traffic from online media buys will end up here. If you don't see much traffic in this report, you are probably not running very substantial online marketing or PR efforts. I recommend you look at Similar Web and find all the referring sites sending traffic to your competitors. Then you can reverse engineer that and use it for your media buys and online PR strategy.

Direct

Direct traffic occurs when people go straight to your website. But they found out about you from somewhere, didn't they? It's usually traditional advertising such as TV or radio. But it can also be digital marketing initiatives that are not being tracked correctly (YouTube ads, display, programmatic, etc.), the result of media exposure or something else. With direct, it is great to see that number going up as it's indicative of a good online presence. When you look at direct traffic, it is always a good idea to see if they are new or returning users. Often, direct goes up for returning users more than new users when a website has a login (think of your bank and how you visit their site to login). It goes up for new users when they are doing advertising, traditional or offline, and don't track it correctly or the user just decides to go right to the URL.

Display

The last channel I will cover is display. Display is right there with affiliate and is usually one of the last places people turn for performance-based marketing, but one of the first places people turn for customer nurturing and awareness. Display generally refers to the Google Display Network, which is the largest in the world, but there are other display networks. When it comes to this channel, start by just using it for remarketing. When remarketing, be deliberate with how you serve the ads to the audience. For example, you might only want to remarket to people who fill out your contact form, hit a service page, or visit a specific product page. Generally, you are going to see a lower ROAS for this channel, so when running it through the Forecaster Method it will be clear you should not be spending too much budget on it initially if you are focused on performance-based marketing initiatives. Display and everything that comes with it is usually where you turn when other channels are saturated but you still want to grow, are continuing to spend using the 10% rule, or are finally to a place where you are looking to raise awareness and even grow a market.

Chapter 10: Conclusion

The Forecaster Method offers marketers a way to make informed decisions about how they market their business. This simple approach to measuring sources of traffic, auditing and establishing the model, forecasting the value, measuring return on ad spend (ROAS), comparing returns, scaling sources to provide business growth based on goals, diversifying for business protection, and continuous optimizing to lower costs is undoubtedly the best way to look at digital marketing, and in my opinion marketing in general.

By taking a mathematical approach and evaluating each channel you're investing in, you can be confident that the money you're investing is helping you reach your business goals.

Furthermore, you can take what you've learned to optimize your entire online and offline sales funnel and improve the channels that aren't seeing the numbers you want.

Once you've run the Forecaster Method on all your traffic sources, use the analytics tools, reports, and insights in this book to help you understand why some of your sources aren't performing as well as others.

Then, once you've optimized the conversion process on each channel, you can create an effective online sales funnel that pushes consumers towards your goal using the steps listed in this book.

As demonstrated in this book, everything works together.

Determine a goal, find an audience, and identify a click-through rate, conversion rate, and value per conversion.

Start running the advertising and consistently improve return on ad spend and gather data.

That data can then be used to improve your website and supplement your other sources and grow.

This is the most exciting time in the history of digital marketing and the Forecaster Method is the system that will bring your company the most success possible.

Using the Forecaster Method, we drive hundreds of leads to Ignite Visibility each month and we have become a 3-time Inc. 5000 company. The Forecaster Method has also helped hundreds of our clients and is the framework we believe in. Now you know the framework for evaluating any advertising in the modern landscape. I hope this brief book helps you spend money wisely, diversify your online portfolio, scale your business to the level you want, and achieve your dreams that come with succeeding in your career, business, and life.

These concepts seem simple, but it is my experience that 99% of businesses do not take the time to properly run this model for all their advertising. They spend, throw money at the wall, and over 50% of the time don't even have a marketing plan. They are lazy, don't care, or simply don't understand and waste money. Use the concepts in this book and you will win.

Now get out there, run the Forecaster Method on your spend, and crush your marketing.

Thank you for being a reader. I believe in Marketing With A Mission and Growth For Good. My business mission is to help others through digital marketing. If this book helped you, I would love to hear about it. Feel free to reach out online.

I want to see you grow and I wish you the best!

Sincerely,

John Lincoln, MBA

CEO of Ignite Visibility

Made in the
USA
Monee, IL